Silly Willy and Silly Billy

Written by Alison Condon   Illustrated by Fraser Williamson

Silly Willy wanted to go for a swim
in the sea.
"It's too cold to swim in the sea,"
said Silly Billy.
So Silly Willy
went for a swim in the bathtub.

Drip, drip, drip went the faucet.
"I will fix that," said Silly Billy,
and he put his toe up into the spout.

"Help! Help!" yelled Silly Billy.
"My toe is stuck in the spout!"

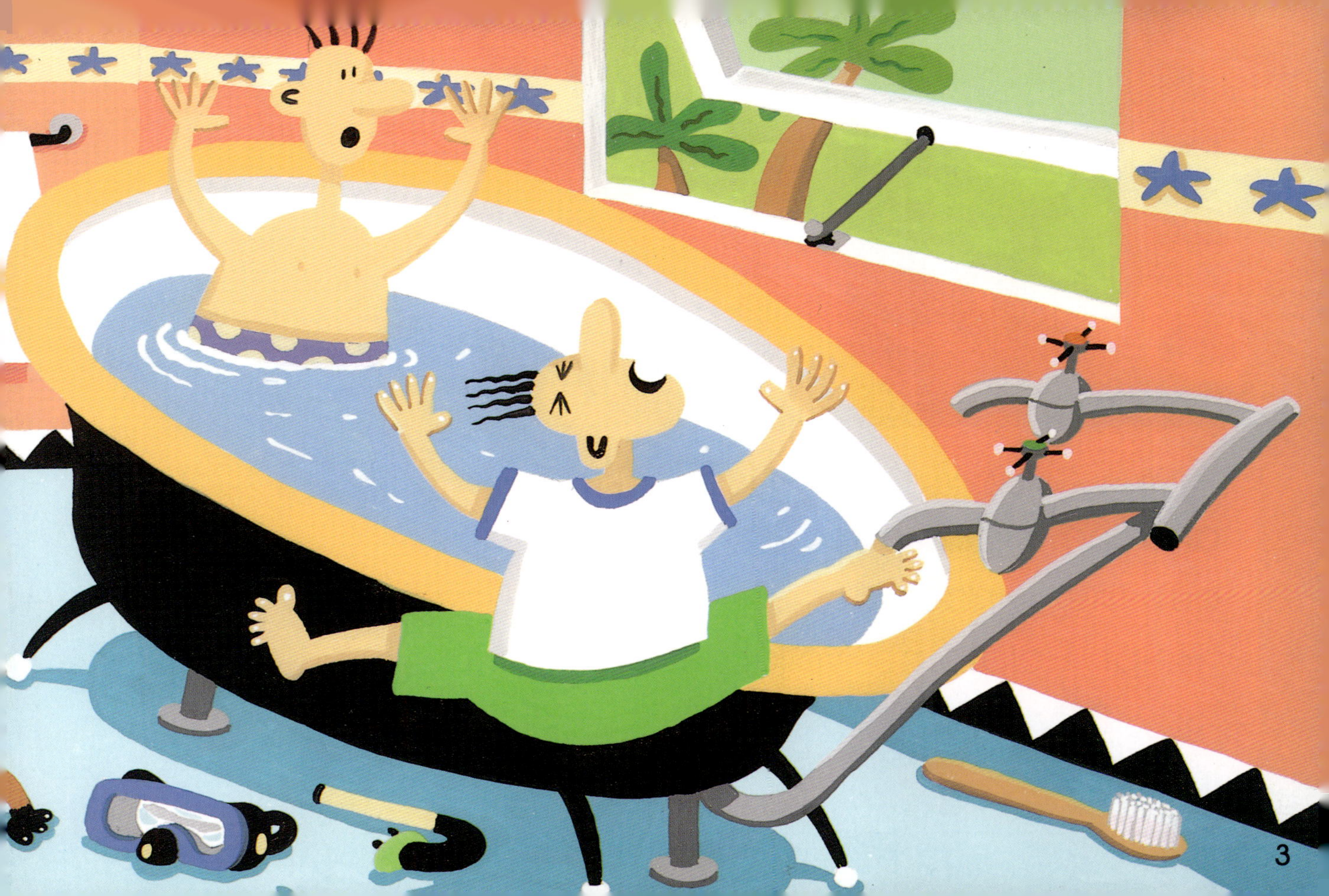

"I will help you," said Silly Willy, and he stuck his head out the window.
"Help! Help!" he yelled.
"Silly Billy's toe is stuck in the spout."

5

"We will help you,"
said the six silly workers.
They put Silly Willy and Silly Billy
and the bathtub onto a big truck.
"Help! Help!" yelled the six silly workers.
"Silly Billy's toe is stuck
in the spout."

7

"I will help you,"
said the silly helicopter pilot.
He lifted Silly Willy and Silly Billy
and the bathtub and the six silly workers
and the truck up into the air.

9

The helicopter went over the rivers
and over the fields.
It went over the hills
and over the beach.
Then the rope went SNAP!
Silly Willy and Silly Billy
and the bathtub and the six silly workers
and the truck fell down into the sea.

11

Silly Billy's toe came out,
and Silly Willy had his swim in the sea!